WALL STREET IS <u>NOT</u> YOUR FRIEND— WATCH OUT!

WEALTH EXPRESS®

Copyright © 2024

All rights reserved.

ISBN-13: 979-8-9915448-2-5

Also by Wealth Express®

The Freedom Protection Plan

For PERMANENT Financial Safety In
Financially Unsafe Times

How To Have Financial CERTAINTY In
Economic Years Ahead,

Even If A "Crash" Comes

Don't Outlive Your Money!

This book is dedicated to Main Street investors,
who put principles before profit.

INTRODUCTION

From the time we're very young, before most kids care about money, our parents tell us about the importance of saving for the future. You gotta save, save, save. And yet…most people don't.

As we grow, enter the workforce, and start to generate income, we're told we not only have to save that money but that we have to put it to work for us. If you're lucky, a parent or mentor warned us you can't save your way to retirement—you must invest. After all, that's how the rich get rich, right? They substitute time with capital. They put their money to work *for* them.

Sounds like a reasonably smart thing to do.

And the rich people do it.

Maybe *I* should too.

So you start to hunt around for smart ways to grow what money you have saved. Often, the first step is taking your company up on the 401(k) they offer. Nice, passive, pre-tax savings and growth, right? Maybe.

Next, you hear about hot stocks your friends, family, and co-workers are "getting in on". That's a good way to score big, right? Maybe.

Finally, you start following business stories online, you see the TV shows on the business news channels. You start to develop a bit of investment sophistication. Enough so that you actually pull the trigger on investments in the stock market or even with real estate. You start to diversify your portfolio. Feels good, right?

Maybe.

Maybe?

Isn't that what you're supposed to do? Isn't that what EVERYONE ELSE IS DOING!!?

That is what everyone else is doing. That is what we are told to do throughout our lives. And yet…50+ million Americans face the very serious, very real threat of outliving their money. They are going to run out of money before they die.

Will you?

Are you sure?

Seems crazy, right? People follow all that

advice, try to "do the right thing", and they still end up wondering, worrying, and working for the rest of their lives? How can that be?

It CAN be because all of that advice that's been followed all of these years all comes from one place: WALL STREET.

The 401(k)s…Wall Street.

The stocks and funds – Wall Street.

The financial news and TV pundits – they're just parroting, and in some cases are owned by, Wall Street.

The sad fact is, most Americans are financially illiterate. They don't know what to do with the money they earn. That creates a gigantic void. So Wall Street comes along and fills that void with what THEY want you to do. See how it works?

Wall Street is more than happy to give you advice, to help you solve a problem they had a hand in creating. Problem is…their advice is advantageous to THEM, not to you. Their advice is designed to make Wall Street richer, not you. If you get rich too, great…they can hit you up for more investments. If their advice steers you wrong and you end up in the poorhouse? Oh well.

It's an endless cycle that leaves most Americans working too long and relaxing too little.

So how are you, the statistical exception, going to avoid the Wall Street mousetrap? It's starts by remembering this:

WALL STREET IS NOT YOUR FRIEND.

But it sure tries to act like it.

The minute you sign up for your first job out of college, you'll probably spend a good hour with the HR representative, who tells you about their amazing 401(k) plan. Great news!…it allows you to invest a portion of your income into any of the zillion different mutual funds from some highly-regarded investment firm. They even dumb those funds down with clever names like *Target Retirement 2050* so you know which one is 'best' for you. It gets better!…because your company will even match how much you invest up to a certain percentage. That's free money! Why wouldn't you take it and make out like a bandit? Forget that rainy day fund. This is your sunny day fund…an easy way to sock away cash for that glorious moment when you leave the office for good, move to Florida, and finally start to LIVE

LIFE!

But ask anyone who was near retirement age between 2008-2010 how reliable a 401(k) investment in the stock market is. That Great Recession hit following the collapse of the housing market. After years of diligently saving, people lost an average of 20% on their 401(k) retirement funds in a just few months.

It wasn't exactly the end of the world for young adults in their 20s, perhaps 30s, whose 401(k)s dropped from $10,000 to $8,000. But for people who had worked longer, saved longer, were older and closer to retirement...it was DEVASTATING.

It's even harder to recover when your 401(k) drops from $800,000 to $600,000. There is not enough time to recover an extra 200 grand that already took a **decade** to accumulate. What if that was you?

That was the catastrophic result for tens of thousands of Americans. Many postponed their retirements by ten years or more. Others had to significantly alter where they were going to work, what their plans would be like, how much (if any) they would travel, what they would do in retirement…who they would BE in retirement. All those 401(k)s are Wall Street products that let Wall Street recover a lot faster than the average American.

In hindsight, it's hard to imagine putting such a significant amount of money into such a risky, vulnerable venture. And yet…here we are a decade-plus later where 401(k)s are still one of the top ways Americans save for retirement.

Stocks keep going up and down like a pogo stick. Problem is…Americans are the suckers getting jerked up and down while Wall Street benefits all the way.

And the TV pundits are like chameleons; ever-changing their reporting to suit the news-room profit center that's funded by ads from….Wall Street. Gaining awareness and tweaking your investing strategy is nice. But I tend to believe once it's announced financial news—it's old news. Do you think the players on Wall Street wait for the TV reports?

Definitely not.

Wall Street LOVES To Gamble... With YOUR Money

Nearly all financial vehicles sold by Wall Street are just different shades of the same basic principle: you gambling your money on things that you don't know that much about or are too complex and confusing for the average retirement-minded investor to act with confidence. Even if you do feel confident, you're still gambling on other people reacting the way that you *think* they should. That's a risky, risky proposition. They are the casino, you are not.

Even then, Wall Street is WAY ahead of all of you. They're driving the market, setting the trends, and making your "hot tip" obsolete before you can make your trade. They hold the edge. And holding the edge requires making sure you don't really ever get the edge.

When I hear someone saying they have a hot tip for the stock market or something that they (or I) can't miss, I think back to my "career" as a sports gambler. I put career in quotes because I've gambled on sports twice in my life, with terrible results. The first time I happened to be in Las

Vegas because it seemed like a fun thing to do. I bet on my college alma mater to cover a 9-½ point spread against their dreaded football rivals. I bet my team would either win or lose by fewer than 10 points. It seemed like a great bet, so I put $100 on it figuring I'd win and end up with a great story…And put $250 in my pocket the next day. A good bet, because I had watched my team play for years and usually the rivalry game was really close.

What happened? **My team lost by 36 points.**

About five years later, I bet on my alma mater again. They were having a terrible season and I was so mad at them that I figured I would bet on them to lose a game, so at least I'd make some money out of their awful campaign. They were playing the #1 team in the country, who were on an 8-game winning streak. My team was a 17-point underdog so I bet on the #1 team to win by at least 18 points.

What happened? **My team beat the #1 team by 4 points.**

That was more than 20 years ago. I learned my lesson. I have no clue how to gamble and gain. Neither do most people, yet they keep frittering money away in investments they simply *have a feeling about*. In fact, I would—ahem—*wager*, that the amount of money lost on investing dwarfs the amount lost to sports gambling and casinos. After all, what's the difference between a Vegas casino and Wall Street? Casinos ADMIT the games are rigged for the house to win. But Wall Street acts like you're their friend.

Wall Street is NOT your friend.

It's never a good idea to gamble your money on something you don't have any control over. But, what's the alternative? The secret sauce to achieving Guaranteed Income for Life? Note the key word there, 'guaranteed'. That's something Wall Street never offers.

Guaranteed Income for Life means safe, certain, secure investing that Wall Street can't deliver. They don't like that idea. They want you to trust them and their investing advice. If only it were a cheap trick. Instead, it's a predatory relationship. And like all abusers, they beat you down to make themselves indispensable.

This book is your way around that chronic, centuries-old snake oil, sweet talkin', "*But it'll work this time!*" dysfunction. This book sets the record straight about Wall Street and your options. This book puts hard-working Americans first, not blue blood, champagne-popping insiders.

Wall Street isn't going to like this book. They're gonna hate it. And that's fine by me. Because your well-being, your happiness without worry during retirement…that's what I care about.

To you and the brightest of futures!

PS – As you continue reading, remember…this book is about one thing and one thing only—giving YOU greater control of YOUR money.

PPS - Yes, there are plenty of good people who work on Wall Street. And it is very likely many of them really do want their clients to succeed. The problem is they all work for the massive Wall Street machine. That machine has only one purpose: to help Wall Street get richer. How do they do that? How do they pile up so much money? **The answer is you.** Let's begin!

1

Breaking Down Wall Street

One of my favorite guilty pleasures is the 1980s NBC miniseries "V". It was an ambitious project that saw aliens arriving on planet Earth in giant spacecrafts. These Visitors looked like us, and other than their odd voices, they seemed peaceful. They promised to help cure our planet's problems—like global warming and cancer.

Everywhere you looked, these aliens were doing outreach programs, internships, giving tours of their spaceships and being our best pals. But there's never a free lunch, is there?

The aliens had ulterior motives. Two of them: 1) Steal our water—their planet ran out a long time ago—and 2) Eat us. Surprise! They were secretly lizard people wearing human masks. All of this came to a head during the conclusion of the first week's episodes, when a human resistor captured the Visitor leader "John" and on national TV declared "The Visitors are NOT our friends!" while tearing off his mask to reveal his green scaly skin underneath. It's hard for me not to feel the same way when I talk to people about the financial analysts up there in New York City.

Wall Street is NOT YOUR FRIEND.

Wall Street does not care if you get rich. Only *their* bank accounts matter. They don't care if you understand the rules of trading. They have their own agenda that you are only part of because they need your money to be successful. That's it. You're like cattle to them if they were in the hamburger business. Sure, they're going to stroke your coat and give you plenty of range to graze. But their real motivation is to fatten you up and get you ready for the slaughter. (Lesson: YOU are Wall Street's meal—you WILL get eaten.)

How Did We Get Here?

If you know American history, or if you've watched *National Treasure* with Nick Cage, you probably know that Wall Street is named because there was a literal wall there. It was built by the Dutch West India Company in 1653 when The Netherlands and England were getting into a war over the colonies. The Dutch, fearing a land invasion of their fancy new island of Manhattan (back then known as New Amsterdam), used slave labor to build a half-mile, 9-foot-tall wall designed to protect this already-important financial center of the colony. And protect it did (as long as you didn't walk all the way to the end of the wall and step around it).

The British never came to Wall Street, but it staved off attacks from Native Americans and pirates over the years. A decade later, the English took over Manhattan and improved the wall considerably. The wall remained up until 1699.

Eventually local merchants and traders started gathering there to move merchandise of all sorts, including the new practices of selling shares in their companies and bonds as well. Those traders eventually formed the Buttonwood Agreement in 1792, the predecessor to the modern New York Stock Exchange. Making sure they got in on the ground floor, the original creators signed an agreement that they would pay a lower commission rate than everyone else. (Lesson: YOU will never be first in line as long as Wall Street's in the picture.)

George Washington was inaugurated there in 1789. The Bill of Rights was also signed on Wall Street. The nearby Trinity Church includes the final resting places of Robert Fulton and Alexander Hamilton. Starting in the early 1800s, more and more businesses moved to Wall Street. And if you had a home there, you got moved out. *Members only, apparently.*

When the Erie Canal opened in the early 19th century, New York City was the only seaport on the Eastern Seaboard with access to the Great Lakes. Business boomed, with more and more businesses rushing to Manhattan. After the Civil War, the country pivoted from agriculture to industrial, and then to financial. Names we still know today like J.P. Morgan and John D. Rockefeller brought their businesses to stay on Wall Street.

In 1884, a man named Charles Dow began tracking the stock prices of 11 companies, mainly railroads, and put together an average platform that he called the *Dow Jones Average*. At the end of the 19th century, the stock report known as the *Customers' Afternoon Letter* became the *Wall Street Journal*, and it started publishing the *Dow Jones Index* in 1896, and has never stopped. Somewhere in the early 20th century, Wall Street started being recognized as the epicenter for the world's financial center, taking the mantle from London.

Most people don't know all that. But most people DO know what happened next, in October 1929.

That was when the famous Yale economist Irving Fisher told everyone that their money was fine on Wall Street despite the market slipping for weeks. A few days after that, the market crashed on October 24, 1929, bringing about the Great Depression. Wall Street was still powerful, but now just as much of a problem as it was an asset in the public consciousness. Regulations soon came to Wall Street for the first time. The government got involved after realizing, more so admitting, how egregious a lot of the deals going down were.

And so the up-and-down roller coaster began. Bull markets, bear markets. More regulation, less regulation. Wall Street could afford an army of lobbyists, to continue tilting the scales in their favor. Ever since then, there has been a long series of highs and lows punctuated by tent pole record days and sinkhole financial collapses wiping out millions of people's retirement savings.

Same Old Story, But Even Worse…

In 1973, the US financial community combined for a loss of $245 million - the equivalent of $1.73 billion in 2024. More reforms were initiated, with the SEC eliminating fixed commissions and eliminating the idea that you could only trade stocks on *the Big Board*, paving the way for electronic transfers. Banks were allowed to buy and sell stocks starting the next year, and more people were able to get into the market.

The 1980s brought recreational drugs to Wall Street, with cocaine becoming a major part of the community, and in 1987, the Dow Jones lost 532 points in a single day, knocking some 100,000 people out of a job.

And Then, Catastrophe…

The 21st century brought near disaster to the New York Stock Exchange on September 11, 2001, when the World Trade Center buildings were attacked by terrorists and destroyed. Some 45% of Wall Street office space was damaged beyond repair, and it closed for a week. The rest of the decade saw high unemployment, falling home costs and enormous national debt, but the people on Wall Street were still healthy and wealthy as ever. How?

Well, because they were furiously trading people's mortgages back and forth like baseball cards, and approving mortgages to people who had no business getting one. Wall Street and banks were making money. But by 2008, the writing was on the wall. The predatory lending and subprime mortgage party came to a crashing halt. Multiple Wall Street investment firms collapsed overnight and the rest had to be bailed out by the federal government.

Did your savings take a hit in 2008? Were YOU bailed out? Of course, not. The American people had no such luck, crashing into the Great Recession as the stock market collapse crushed thousands of dreams and devalued 401(k) funds and other financial instruments.

And yet…Wall Street has continued to provide an endless list of "hot tips" since then.

2

How Wall Street Makes Their Money

You may not realize it, but Wall Street makes money off the back of investors in several ways:

Brokerage Commissions:

Every time you buy or sell a stock, a bond, a mutual fund, or any security with the help of a brokerage firm, you'll pay a fee to them for executing the trade. Every single time. It doesn't matter if you are selling 500 shares, 5 million shares, or 5 shares, you're paying a commission determined by your brokerage house. Yep, they're making money whether you're spending it or making it. That's pretty brilliant. It's also ruthless. As we move through this book you'll notice that's always their MO. If you ask a broker, "why all the fees?", they'll tell you that you're paying for their advice, knowledge and research. So in their words, you're paying their salary.

Assets Management Fees:

This fee is for a brokerage firm to watch over your account - including stocks, bonds, mutual funds, ETFs and whatever else you own. Management fees are usually based on the amount of assets you have under management - so in this instance, Wall Street wants you to as many as possible. You might be asking yourself, shouldn't all those brokerage commissions be included in my asset management fees?

Yes, you are learning quickly about Wall Street! Buying and selling your assets sounds like something that would fall under the umbrella of asset management. But Wall Street figures, *"Why not make them two separate things at double the price?"* It's also pretty irksome knowing that the value of your assets could have absolutely nothing to do with anything the brokerage company is doing—but they still benefit from your success.

It works like this: You might wake up on January 1st and decide to invest $50,000 in Stock A, and then never make another move for the rest of the year. But if you started with $50,000 in Stock A, and on December 31, Stock A is now worth $300,000, you better believe your investment broker will charge a big fat commission on that $300,000 that they had nothing to do with.

Financial Advisory Services:

When you enroll with a brokerage account, you may be the beneficiary of financial advisory services—whether you want them or not. Some are part of your package deal, some are an added fee if you want the good stuff. Other times, they give you a free trial that is very hands-on and makes you feel valued and like it's essential. Then after 30, 60, or 90 days, the free luxury services you've *just* gotten used to go away…unless you want to pay for them. If you have a sharp eye, you're probably wondering why this fee gets charged—when you're supposedly already paying for their financial advice as part of the brokerage commission. Well, it's because these guys really like money, and they love YOUR money even better. They want your money to come to them, and then it's their money. And the easiest way to do that is put all these fees in place—that they don't mention until you're just about done signing up. And at that point it's more convenient to bite the bullet than to start all over somewhere else.

It's the same shtick as when you're in the final stages of buying a car. You've hammered out the price and monthly payment, and now you're in that tiny office signing reams of paper when suddenly all the fees come up…now you're paying an extra $1,200 for nothing tangible or nothing you want. *"Didn't we tell you? Your car has our exclusive, premium pinstriping and it can't be removed. So what's a couple hundred dollars amongst friends?"* Some of it is legit for the car dealership because you're taking out a loan and there are a lot of hoops to jump through. That's not the case with financial services. You're just paying them for things they already know. If it wasn't so rotten it would be sort of brilliant.

Underwriting and Investment Banking:

If you own a small business you probably are familiar with the idea of raising capital, issuing debt, making second offers, and even initial public offerings (IPOs). These items don't have much to do with most investors, it's more of an idea of the big banks realizing they could make more money by offering more services, which of course they also charge fees on.

Market-making and Trading:

Wall Street creates new markets, new securities, advertises them, and then facilities trading activities for buyers and sellers. They earn money through the process of bid-ask spreads, which is the difference between the asking price and the selling price.

Proprietary Trading:

Proprietary trading is when Wall Street firms trade securities they hold themselves in order to make profits. It does not involve any individual investors. This can be done to relieve bad quarters or months or years, or it can be done when a firm is getting ready to make a big move, like the acquisition of another company.

As you can see, Wall Street has stacked the deck on how it makes money, with and without you. The investment firms have gradually expanded what they offer. Many are now one-stop shops offering everything an individual investor or a business needs when it comes to the financial markets. That gives them an outrageous amount of power and you almost none. But don't worry, we can fix that.

3

Wall Street's Greatest Lies

Wall Street has told some real whoppers over the years. Mistruths, fact-fudging, outright lies—in an attempt to move more money from Main Street to Wall Street. There was the housing crisis mentioned in the last chapter where, suddenly, people who had never lived in a house before were approved for massive amounts of money for homes they could never afford, or second mortgages to buy fancy cars that were not in the budget. They got behind on payments, defaulted on mortgages, and the banks suddenly owned a zillion houses they didn't want and couldn't pay the mortgages on.

Ten years before that, Wall Street wanted you to know that any company with a .com was the next greatest thing ever and you should throw as much money as possible at their stocks. That bubble burst too, and you probably recall how painful it was.

But those are short-term lies. The real doozies are the ones that Wall Street is constantly preaching to anyone who will listen, although their favorite targets are senior citizens and people fresh out of college entering the workforce. Let's take a look at a few of Wall Street's Greatest (Worst) hits.

Lie #1: Getting In The Stock Market and Staying There Long-Term is the Way to Go.

If you're reading this, and you can't remember what the Y2K scare was all about because you were a baby or hadn't been born yet, then yes, the stock market is a proven long-term investment.

Over time, like several decades, you are more likely to make money than lose it. But that requires leaving your money the entire time, not freaking out, and hoping and praying that when you do decide to cash out something terrible isn't happening.

Imagine you started working at a company in 1980 and you had 2020 as your target retirement date. You're ready to start sectioning out all your 401(k) and other accounts you've saved up to wipe out the rest of your mortgage, pay off your debts, and start some easy living, while keeping a nice chunk of money in the market. Then just months after you've retired you hear about some weirdo flu killing people in China. Three weeks later, it's here, you're terrified for your life, and the Dow Jones drops 3,800 points in 5 days, making that 532-point decline back in 1987 seem like a day at the beach.

Here's my point: If you're older or if your financial needs are immediate, then you should steer well clear of the stock market. For starters, when the market takes a big downturn, and then goes up by the same amount the next year, that's not the same thing as getting all of your money back.

How does that work? Well, let's run the numbers. Say you've got $1,000,000 in your 401(k) and when you're 60 years old the market suddenly takes a 25% hit because of a secondary strain of COVID arising. Just like that, you're out $250,000 and down to $750,000 entering the new year. Things rebound as they usually do and the market rises 15% next year, and 10% the year after that. You've made your money back! Right?

Well, no, not even close. Those percentages look good on paper, but that's the kind of question that you're going to blow your good SAT score on. When we run the numbers, starting at $750,000 and the year that has a 15% return, that means your total asset amount goes up to $862,500. Then the market goes up 10% next year, and you make it back to $948,750. That's not $1 million though is it? That's $51,250 short. That's a year's payments of a really nice mortgage, or getting yourself out of credit card debt, or buying your spouse a new car on their 50th birthday. And that's on top of the earnings your lost money would have generated.

You don't—and can't—control the market, right? The loss isn't your fault. **But it is your problem.** Wall Street would tell you not to worry, "the market will bounce back". But what if you're retired? What if you're in your Golden Years? What are you supposed to do then?

Stock market risk is a younger person's game. They have more time to recover and often less to lose, but you do not. They don't have decades of earnings, savings, and growth on the line. But you do. And one more stock market "oopsie" could mean your standard of living, your comfort in retirement, could suffer a drastic discount markdown for the rest of your life.

Even if your money was able to bounce back to break even, is the stress and worry about watching the market swing up and down worth it? You have to be prepared to feel the gut-wrenching pain of losing 20-30% of your nest egg, in real time. That will never feel good.

We're not talking **risk tolerance** here; we're talking LOSS TOLERANCE. There's obviously a big difference between the two. **Risk tolerance** means exactly what it sounds like—*how much risk are you willing to take? How exposed are you willing to get?* Risk tolerance says, "I'm OK if this $10,000 never grows bigger than $10,000, or even drops to $7,500 or $5,000 before I sell."

Loss tolerance is different because it means you're OK with that amount of money going away, going completely to zero…and never coming back. Saying you're OK with your $1,000 turning into $800 (20% loss) is a lot easier than saying the same thing when it's $500,000 turning into $400,000. Saying it when you're 60 is a lot different than saying it when you're 30.

So be honest with yourself. What amount of money is a fair amount to disappear forever? I don't know a lot of people who go above even 10%, much less 20-30%.And when you're retired, EVERY penny counts.

Even investing only in big name, blue-chip companies isn't a safety net. Companies like Dow or General Mills or P&G, Coke and Disney, have proven resilient. So far. Would you ever have thought Walgreens, with their stores on virtually every corner of America filled with must-have items like Medicine, would face a rapid 24% stock price crash? IT CAN HAPPEN. Bad things DO happen to good stocks!

Target is another stable, very well-respected company. They have a strong brand identity, more upscale than Walmart but still not killing you with the highest prices. They've made a fortune bringing high design to the masses. You can buy necessities such as clothing and groceries there. Back in the 2010s, Target was chugging right along on its way up, after the Great Recession. By the time 2014 ended, it had scored positive returns in five of the past six years, including a very nice 19.98% in 2014. At the end of 2014, Target suffered from HVAC-Gate conveniently at Christmas time, the most profitable time of the year. Usually.

But Christmas 2014 was like none other for Target. A glitch in the system allowed hackers to use stolen credentials from a third-party vendor to obtain the credit and debit card information from a staggering 40 million customers in the span of just 18 days. It wasn't some sophisticated swindling. The screw-up was the result of Target giving an HVAC company that serviced its grocery freezers unlimited access to its servers holding invoice, billing, and property management details.

Crook(s) stole those credentials from the HVAC company and feasted on the results. Investigations revealed that Target had missed dozens of alarms from its cybersecurity mainframe warning that suspicious activity was going on. By the time the dust settled, the company's reputation was tarnished and the CEO and CIO both resigned. Target stock fell 4.35% in 2015, 0.52% in 2016, and 9.66% in 2017. A dark triple whammy from a company most assume would be a lead-pipe cinch to consistently make money.[1]

We're all good at taking things for granted. We presume some things will simply be around forever. But where are the indestructible Sears, Newspapers, and Cable TV today? I still can't believe we now have multiple generations of youth who DON'T KNOW THE BEATLES!

Change is inevitable and always brings risk. With the sprawl of (uncontrolled, unrestricted) technology shoving its way into every aspect of our lives, change is accelerating. With that comes an ever-increasing chance of making investment mistakes.

Then there's the idea of the safety of mutual funds or ETFs (Exchange-Traded Funds). These can be thought of as a basket of securities that all are somehow related, usually under a heading like Tech Startups or Bio-Friendly or something like that. The problem with both of these is that they are usually top heavy, meaning there's two or three proven winners in the mix and the rest are just companies that fall into the same category. It's like selling you a book of coupons where your absolutely favorite restaurant is on the cover, but everything else isn't so great.

Lie #2: Dividend-Paying Stocks Give Me A Guaranteed Income

Dividends are to investors what a fishing lure is to a 15-pound rainbow trout--bright, shiny, appealing. But once you're hooked, things don't always go great. The biggest misconception is thinking that all dividend stocks are the same; they're not. In a nutshell, stock dividends are payments that the company makes to its shareholders as a reward for their investments. They either come as cash or as additional shares of stock. Most people choose to either take the payments in cash or to reinvest them straight into their holdings with the company. But those dividends are just as volatile as a stock's prices over the year and over many years.

An example: This quarter, you might get $500 as a dividend. Next quarter you might get $33.12. The quarter after that, you might get nothing. There is literally no guarantee at all. Companies are often listed by their dividend yield, which is a ratio that measures the annual dividends it pays relative to its stock price. In theory, you want a high dividend yield because it means more money for you. But most investors shy away from stocks with a high dividend yield because as the stock price goes down, the dividend yield goes up. If you have a $100 stock that pays a $2 annual dividend for a yield of 2%, what happens if the dividend stays the same but the price drops to $50. Now your dividend yield is $4, but the stock is significantly devalued, meaning its overall value has been cut in half. It's deceiving.

Lie #3: Municipal Bonds Are A SAFE, Tax-Free, Wise Investment

On the surface, municipal bonds sound like a dream come true. They are exempt from federal taxes and are a fairly low-risk investment. Cities sell them when they want to raise money for a big project, like a sports arena, a revitalized downtown, or anything else that is in the public's interest.

There are a number of not-so-obvious negatives to consider, however. First, the interest rate paid by municipal bonds is lower than rates on corporate bonds. So if you're looking to clean up on this investment, you're going the wrong way. There's also the risk that the interest rate on the bonds will drop, and that risk increases the longer the bond's term. If you invest in a 20-year municipal bond, who knows what the interest rate will look like at the end of that term?

You also have to worry about the *callable options* of a bond. That means the issuer can cancel the issue, pay off the remaining principal, and stop making interest payments. Most municipal bonds have that function because it allows them to take advantage of interest rate drops, which would give municipalities the opportunity to open a new bond at a lower rate. They'll be happy to offer it to you again, now new and "improved" with the opportunity to make even less money. Isn't that nice of them?

Although historically quite low, there is also the risk of default. The last time that happened was in 2022 with a student housing project. Rare, but it does and CAN happen. And when you look around the US today, there are clearly many cities struggling with internal problems that make them a risk to pay back their debts. Keep that in mind when you look at the name on the bond. Are you prepared to gamble your retirement lifestyle on the changing winds of some city's economic forecast?

Lie #4: Investments Equal Income

The investment types we're talking about here

are all gambles, plain and simple. They might be better gambles than your odds of winning the Powerball or Harvard beating Alabama, but they are still gambles. Because no matter how much information or insight you have, you can't know what will happen with the price of any particular financial instrument from one day to the next. *Not even the pros know.* You might make a small profit or get dividend income every year, but the odds are so low you'll never be able to do so consistently. While the average S&P 500 rate of return has been 10% yearly dating back to 1928, the times that it has been between 10.00%-10.99% can be counted on one hand. Just twice in fact: 10.26% in 1949 and 10.79% in 1971[2]. The rest of the last 96 years, it's been anyone's guess and taken some wild swings.

Here are a few examples to think about:

In the middle of the Great Depression, there were two huge return years: 41.37% in 1935 and 27.92% in 1936. But it all fell apart in 1937, when the federal government took some big swings and global peace was threatened by increasing aggression from Germany. The S&P had a return rate of 38.59% in 1937, followed by four years out of five with negative returns.

The 80s were the best, right? The S&P had its

best all-time streak from 1982-1989, eight straight years of positive returns. Then in 1990, a crazy guy named Saddam Hussein decided he needed Kuwait's oil all for himself and invaded one random night in August. It plunged the US and the UN into the Gulf War and sent oil prices skyrocketing. In 1989, the S&P was up 27.25% and in 1991 it was up 26.31%. But smack-dab in the middle was -6.56% in 1990.

2008's Mortgage Crisis Crash yielded a -38.49% return, the third-highest drop in history. It came after five straight years of positive returns.

The bottom line is the market is too volatile and too dependent on an overwhelming list of unforeseeable events, to think you'll get the same positive return year after year.

[1] www.1stock1.com. (n.d.). *TGT: Target Corporation Yearly Stock Returns.* [online] Available at: https://www.1stock1.com/1stock1_246.htm [Accessed 27 June. 2024].

[2] CMT, C.M. (2022). *Average Historical Stock Market Returns for S&P 500 (5-year up to 150-year averages).* [online] Trade That Swing. Available at: https://tradethatswing.com/average-historical-stock-market-returns-for-sp-500-5-year-up-to-150-year-averages/.

4

TRYING TO INVEST ALL BY YOURSELF

Ever since our founding nearly 250 years ago, America and Americans have had *do-it-yourselfism* in their blood. Doing it yourself IS great. Succeeding by yourself boosts pride and confidence. Home Depot proves and profits handsomely from this very notion. They also make a TON of money off of unskilled amateurs doing it wrong, burning through materials, over-buying supplies, and splurging on showpiece tools that they only use once a year…if they're consistent.

Knowing this, knowing all about Home Depot's rookie mistake revenue, Wall Street has been kind enough to give Americans tools to invest for themselves. Digital investing platforms, self-select benefits packages, choose your own 401(k) adventures, and so on.

How do you think that's going to turn out?

Even if you do pick a few winners, there are many pitfalls that await your independent investing. Here are three of the biggest ways to get yourself in a whole lot of trouble…

#1: The Retirement Tax Bomb

Saving for retirement and putting money into traditional financial vehicles might look great on the surface, but when you hit 65 or whatever your retirement age is going to be, you might easily run into financial disaster when you start moving money around. If you haven't properly accounted for taxes related to your retirement savings, you're perilously close to triggering the ***Retirement Tax Time Bomb.***

The government requires that you start withdrawing money at certain points from your account after you retire. And if you miss the deadline, you get penalized. If you miss even one withdrawal period, you can punish yourself with these huge penalties. The amount you have to take is determined by what is called the *Fair Market Value (FMV)* of the account from the previous year and mixed with your life expectancy. So not only are they making you take your money out, but they're also basing it on how soon they think you're going to die. Aren't they a ray of sunshine!

These mandates are in place whether you used a 401(k) or other workplace plan, or if you went with a Roth IRA where you paid the taxes upfront. Yep, that's exactly what it sounds like, even though you already paid the taxes upfront on these investments, you're still going to be penalized if you don't take them out by a certain date. Trust me, I could write another entire book solely on Free Frustrations. And maybe I should, Because an astonishing number of people go into retirement completely blind to all the nit-picking navigation required to take back YOUR money.

I'll presume you're smart enough to figure some of these things out on your own. But do you honestly have the bandwidth for that? Is that how you want to spend your time and energy?

#2 The Market Crashes Will Kill You

If you didn't get the hint from the last chapter, here it is in big bold letters: THE STOCK MARKET WILL FALTER AND YOU WILL GET BURNED.

It doesn't matter how diverse your portfolio is or how many different positions you maintain. When the market crashes, everything tumbles. As I showed in our opening chapter, losing 25% of your net worth this year, then earning back 25% over the next two years is not an equal sum equation.

The average American lost 30-40% of their 401(k) value in 2008's journey to the *Great Recession*. Let's imagine you were 60 years old that year and had saved $2 million in your 401(k). Suddenly, 40% of that was gone by the end of the year, knocking you down to $1.2 million to start 2009, barely halfway above where you had been 365 days before.

Assuming you got the exact same return as the S&P 500, your value increased 23.45% in 2009. That gets you up to $1.48 million. The market went back up 12.78% in 2010. Now you're at 1.67 million entering 2011.

But 2011 had a rate of return of 0%. So now we're four years past the 40% collapse and you're still $333,000 shy of your original figure.

In 2012, the rate of return was 13.41%. That gets you to $1.89 million. Then 2013 is a really big year, a 29.6% increase, which gets you to a whopping $2.45 million. If you were 60 in 2008, that means you were probably going to retire in 2013, and here you are, finally above your original number again. All's well that ends well, right?

Well, no, not even a little bit. The $2 million you were at in 2008 wasn't supposed to be the ceiling of your retirement income. It's just where you were for one fixed moment in time. You were operating under Wall Street's oldest rule in the book, which says that you'll average a return of 10% PER YEAR if you invest in the S&P 500. If we add up the six years between 2008 and 2013 and divide it by 6, we get an average yearly return of 6.79%. The chasm between 6.79% and 10% is significant to you, right?

And that's not even the biggest point here.

If you were guaranteed an average rate of return, let's talk about what your worth should be in 2013. If you were at $2 million in 2008 and got 10% every year, your worth would expand to:

- $2.2 million in 2009
- $2.42 million in 2010
- $2.66 million in 2011
- $2.93 million in 2012
- $3.22 million in 2013

The math is painful. If you had that expected rate of return instead of what really happened, you would have an additional $771,000. This is the perfect proof that the only way to survive a market crash is to have decades to catch up. Most people don't have decades.

Do you?

#3 Even Government Bonds have Risks

Every investment has risks, even the ones that pretend they don't. Most call US Treasury bonds a risk-free investment, which makes sense because the US government has never defaulted on a debt or missed a payment in its 250-year history. But the risk (opportunity cost) is that the money you put into a treasury bond or another government financial instrument might have had a much better rate of return somewhere else. If you had the opportunity to put $100 into a T-bond that pays 2.5% interest or into a stock that makes a 20% return over the same amount of time, you might not see it as a risk, but you definitely missed out on the opportunity to make more money. Other risks or government bonds include:

Inflation: If you're reading this in 2024, you know all about. If the inflation rate exceeds the rate of return on your bond investment, then by the time you get it back, it will be worth less than when you bought it—based on the purchasing power of the principal. If you put $1,000 in a T-bond for a year at 1% interest, then you wind up with $1,010 a year later. But if inflation at the time is 2%, then the money you get back has a buying power that is only worth $990. Not good.

As we talked about in the last chapter, you can also get burned by a call from the initiator of the bond. If the government extends an offer for loans at 4% interest and you buy in, you imagine you'll be notching those 4% interest payments every month or quarter until the cows come home. But when the Fed lowers interest rates and the government entity realizes it can get away with a 2.5% interest rate, all of a sudden, they're dumping you out of the way, giving you that principal back, and shorting your investment payments. Not cool. But they make the rules.

5

The Real Solution to Generating Guaranteed Income for Life

That's three whole chapters…just to cover the problems with Wall Street and the error of presuming they have your best interests at heart. Three chapters—that's a lot of problems! Even with all that background, chances are you already suspected Wall Street is at best incredibly disappointing and at worst simply up to no good.

So how do you fight it? How do you protect yourself, your nest egg, your retirement?

What IS the solution?

Let's cut right to it. It's *very hard* to trust anyone these days. People use words and phrases and images to mean all sorts of things other than the truth, particularly since the Internet became so important in our lives. It can really be tough to convince someone of how good an idea is for them, because we're all so used to being scammed left and right. It stinks, but it's reality.

I say this because I am very aware that the phrase Guaranteed Income for Life sounds a bit sensational. Like the kind of thing you'd see on a TV infomercial at 3 in the morning. Not only that people often confuse the Guaranteed Income For Life Plan with the guaranteed universal income plan being tested for the government. The two are not the same.

Nevertheless, I use the term Guaranteed Income for Life for two reasons.

First, it starts a conversation. Sometimes, it's a conversation that begins with heavy skepticism, but that's okay. Unlike a lot of people pitching their own ideas, I don't expect you to automatically believe what I'm saying. I hope you will not! I want you to explore the space for yourself, poke holes in what I'm saying and really test my knowledge. Why? Because nobody should invest their money in a product that they don't fully understand and don't 100% believe in.

However, I *understand* the methodology behind the Guaranteed Income for Life plan, and I can explain it to anyone, from any walk of life, with any education level, because it never changes. That's comforting.

Things change too much too fast in this world for a lot of people. I remember driving around with my kids once and them asking what had changed the most since I was their age. Looking around outside the car, it didn't seem that much was different until I considered things like *DoorDash*, a GPS map on my phone, or how there are almost no travel agent storefronts, and about a million other things. But the methodology behind a Guaranteed Income for Life plan has **stood the test of time**.

The second reason for that name is because its benefit is *in the name*. With a Guaranteed Income

For Life Plan, guaranteed income for the rest of your life IS exactly what you get. Definitively. Proven. Guaranteed. This isn't a gimmick, it's a tool that you can use to conservatively grow your retirement money with guaranteed returns, zero risk of losing your principal, and if you choose, a retirement paycheck delivered to you every single month for the rest of your life.

That's the guarantee. If you believe the only guarantees are death and taxes, I appreciate this opportunity to convince you otherwise. So let's get to the meat and potatoes!

The guarantee in this plan is that once you've invested your principal, the stock market's fluctuations will never hurt you. That's because this plan is tied to a fixed market index, not to the actual market. That's a crucial difference.

The Guaranteed Income for Life plan is brilliant because it grows your investment on a tax-deferred basis and it gives you the opportunity to earn a guaranteed lifetime withdrawal benefit *(GLWB)*.

The *GLWB* is the fixed amount that you will receive from your account every month. Your retirement paycheck. You will define what that amount is at the beginning of the investment, meaning YOU decide how much is withdrawn based on YOUR needs. This is significantly different from the mandatory withdrawals the government demands.

That might sound like it's too good to be true, but it is not! Remember, you aren't dealing with a stockbroker in this process; your partner here is a life insurance company. They're the Steady Eddie of financial institutions. Unlike Wall Street, they don't like risks. Unlike banks that only have to keep 10% of their clients' money in-house, insurance companies have to keep 100+% of their clients' money in-house. And unlike just about any other investment…when you sign an agreement for a Guaranteed Income For Life plan, they sign it too. That locks them in, and that means:

They are contractually obliged to pay you the return on your investment they promise.

They are contractually obliged to protect your principal.

They are contractually obliged to send your retirement paycheck each month.

With Wall Street, YOU are on the hook. With a Guaranteed Income For Life plan, the *insurance company* issuing the plan is on the hook. Not YOU.

Remove the risk. Lock in the return. Receive steady income—that's safe, smart, conservative investing.

"If it's so conservative, how do I make money?"

I'll tell you. Insurance companies use what is called the participation rate. The participation rate is a fixed mathematical formula that allows your fund to continue growing over time in a way that benefits not only you, but the insurance company as well. The participation rate measures how much of the return on the fund you are going to keep every year.

Let's say the participation rate in your Guaranteed Income for Life plans is 50%. That means for every dollar that the fund returns over the course of the year, you get 50% of it and the other 50% is invested back into the fund. So if the fund makes a return of 22% of the year, you get 11% of that money and the fund gets the other 11%.

To compare it to something more tangible: think about a joint business venture. Let's say you supplied 10% of the original cost to get the business going, and the deal was that you get 10% of the profits going forward in perpetuity. That means that when a client orders $100 worth of merchandise, you get $10 of that $100, and the rest goes to the other partners. $10 out of $100 might not seem like a lot, but consider that you're receiving it without actually doing anything.

You've done the work with your initial investment, and every sale that happens from now on is going to contribute directly to your bottom line. If you were more involved in the business, you could probably demand a higher share of the profits, but it also might mean that some years you'd be doing a lot more work with no guarantee that you were going to make a lot more money.

Let me be clear: Regardless of how the market performs, you will still receive your guaranteed return from the insurance company. If the market tanks, you will receive your guaranteed return. If the market skyrockets, you will receive your guaranteed return and, possibly more. That depends on the plan you get. Your Wealth Express® Certified Advisor can show you all of your best options.

Dealing with insurance companies instead of as opposed to financial analysts is a unique way to help secure your financial future. They are much less susceptible to the aches and pains of the economy. By their very nature, they are much more stable than financial companies. There's never a time when people don't need insurance, which is why they can be confident in their rate of return and guarantees.

Yes, giant downturns in the stock market will limit their year-to-year rate of return, but they are operating off a massive pool of customers who are perpetuating the principal. A downturn would have to last for more than a decade for insurance companies to even struggle to pay out their guaranteed rates. The more likely scenario is that your money stays protected and your retirement remains stable. Here are four reasons why:

Guaranteed Income:

Let's face it, everything you do in retirement will have ripple effects. You have to be careful when and how much you draw out of your IRA and 401(k) accounts because you're going to have to pay taxes on them. There could be a costly emergency requiring the use of saved funds, medical or otherwise. We all know someone who has had to face this type of expensive challenge. Then there's the inconsistency of Social Security payments. Nobody can tell you how much you're going to get until you've actually retired. And the fact is you can earn nearly $100K EXTRA if you delay taking your Social Security income. Some people are cashing out the minute they get to age 62 so they can get at least 70% of their benefit and hope that it holds out while they get closer and closer to the full benefit age, which as of right now is 67 years old. Of course if you're in your 50s right now, by the time you get to 67, the new benchmark might be 71 or 74. The bottom line is that it's not a source of revenue you can readily count on.

But your Guaranteed Income For Life plan CAN deliver you stable, reliable income every month. That's something you can budget around. That's one solid stepping-stone of stability for your retirement. That's how to make sure you do not outlive your money. A serious consideration considering how advanced our medicines are getting and how they are prolonging lifespan. In fact, Medical researchers say the first person to live to be 200 years old *has already been born.*

The question is not, 'How long will you live?'. The real question is, "I might live longer than expected so how do I make sure I have plenty of money for the ride?" The answer to that question is a Guaranteed Income For Life plan. Because if you retire at 65 and start receiving your monthly payments, it doesn't matter if you are 75, 85, 95, or 105, you're still going to be receiving them as long as you keep on being a resident of Planet Earth.

Tax Benefits:

It's really simple. In a 401(k), your savings can get taxed 3 separate times before it passes along to your family; a Guaranteed Income For Life plan is taxed just once. Any conservative worth their salt knows minimizing taxes is just. Every retiree knows minimizing taxes is ESSENTIAL to extending the life of your retirement savings.

No Contribution Limit:

We conservative-minded people don't like to be told what we can and cannot do with our hard-earned money. For a 401(k), you can't contribute more than between $23,000-30,000 per year. For IRAs, the number is a ridiculously low $7,000 per year. If you've ever wondered why some people don't end up with enough to live on in retirement, you could point a finger right at these limitations. But you can invest what you want into a Guaranteed Income For Life plan, and put more money to work for you. Yes, Wall Street WILL let you invest as much money as you like. They encourage it. But we both know they have ulterior motives. Plus, they don't guarantee a return or zero-risk protection for your principal.

Peace of Mind:

You can't put it on a sheet of paper or store it in a vault, but any investment vehicle that can give you more peace of mind should be seriously considered. When you have a Guaranteed Income for Life plan as part of your Freedom Protection Plan®, and you're receiving your monthly retirement paycheck from it…you feel more secure, more at ease. Because you know…that check will arrive every month, on time.

It will pair perfectly with your Social Security income, as well as your pension if you have one, dividends and other investment returns. You will have money every month. As if you were still working…but without having to do all the work. What happens to money worries then? For the most part, they evaporate. Of course, you didn't put yourself into a position to invest by NOT paying attention to money. But with this plan, it won't be a pressing issue. Money anxiety won't wake you up at night. Your retirement budget will be under control. Your peace of mind will be locked in. What a difference!

There is something to be said for that kind of consistency. A pact, where both parties live up to their side of the agreement. Results you can set your watch by. Stability on which you can build your long-term financial well-being…so you can enjoy the retirement you have earned over decades of work. That seems awfully UN-Wall Street, doesn't it?

Call 833-600-2832 now

to schedule your FREE Retirement Risk Assessment Meeting with a Wealth Express® Certified Advisor.

WSA 131

6

LIES ABOUT GUARANTEED INCOME FOR LIFE

Wall Street has one heck of a spin machine. It's big and loud. They crank it up when they want to sell you something—and crank it louder when they don't want you sending your money somewhere else. That's their response to Guaranteed Income For Life plans. Wall Street DOES NOT LIKE THEM. Why? Those plans provide what Wall Street doesn't want to—a guaranteed return on a protected principal.

And so...the Wall Street spin machine goes to work. Here are some of the big lies they tell about Guaranteed Income For Life plans...

LIE #1 - You Are Robbed Of Opportunities For Market Gains – Which Can Be BIG!

Mom & Dad told us, *"You can't have your cake and eat it too."* That's true, for the most part. Your financial safety DOES involve some trade-off. Guaranteed Income For Life plans are NOT the flashy red sports car investment most investors dream about. They are not the swing-for-the-fences-and-hope-for-a-home-run investment wildcat investors throw money at in hopes of having life-changing money rain down upon them. You WILL have to forego the high risks and high costs of what the kids call FOMO, the Fear Of Missing Out.

With a Guaranteed Income For Life plan, you give up the very slim possibility of double-digit home run returns IN EXCHANGE FOR ZERO RISK to your principal and a modest guaranteed return. You sacrifice improbability for

CERTAINTY. You make a safe bet, and a safe bet is a good bet. Always. Especially when there is little to no time to recover from getting wiped out swinging at the hard-dip knuckleball "hot tip" you thought for sure was going to be a home run. The money you invest in a Guaranteed Income For Life plan is COMPLETELY PROTECTED from market losses you can't recover from.

LIE #2 - Annuities Are BAD Investment Products.

That depends on why you're investing. If you are looking to knock one out of the park as described above, maybe annuities aren't your best choice. BUT…annuities make GREAT Guaranteed Income investment products. And Guaranteed Income is what every retiree needs. Because when your active earning stops, the way you invest and the reason why you invest MUST change. There's a new objective—growth and preservation. And you gotta stick the landing. Fixed Index Annuities, the muscle behind Guaranteed Income For Life plans have ZERO downside risk. Your principal stays intact. AND YET…there may even be some upside and a share of the gains.

Annuities are backed by more diversified investing than you could ever do on your own. They are backed again…by giant, REGULATED, rated insurance companies. Warren Buffett is a fan of such companies *because they get paid up front and are masters at assessing risk*. They are careful and deliberate. Enough so they are willing to guarantee your return and your principal…Will Wall Street do that?

Safe, steady, certain. This frees you up from being a Dow-Watcher. This lets you set-it-and-forget-it. Nothing else provides such a SOLID FOUNDATION for retirement.

And consider this…

You have life insurance for when you die. This, Guaranteed Income For Life, is like having WAY OF LIFE insurance, for the entire time you are still alive, while you can still enjoy it. It ensures your WAY OF LIFE is protected by delivering you a retirement paycheck—steady, dependable income—each and every month.

LIE #3 - Annuities Have Fees And Commissions, And That's Bad

ALL investment products have fees and

commissions. There is nothing wrong with a high commission —it is your GUARANTEED payout that matters to you. Why? If you've seen these companies on TV advertising that they take no commission and *"We only do better when our clients do better,"* they're using sleight of hand. What they don't tell you is that instead they're going to take a set percentage OFF THE TOP of all your money they manage. They're going to take their commission first, before it has a chance to lose money. Because why would they want to short themselves?

And these off-the-top percentages can run to $500K MINIMUM. Of course, they're going to skip the commission when they can take that kind of money regardless of whether or not they are successful. At least with annuities, fees and commissions are TRANSPARENT & FULLY DISCLOSED. Now, consider this. Wall Street pays HUGE, HUGE bonuses and commissions on EVERYTHING it sells to investors, NOT CUSTOMERS. And they are NOT always transparently disclosed.

Annuities Have Been Trusted for, Well, a VERY LONG TIME. As in...

Annuities in Ancient Rome trace their origins to the concept of "annua," a financial instrument that allowed individuals to secure a steady stream of income in exchange for a lump-sum payment. The development of annuities is often attributed to the Roman jurist *Gaius*, who lived during the 2nd century AD. Gaius and other Roman legal scholars formalized the concept of annuities, embedding the idea into Roman financial and legal systems. The motivation behind creating annuities was to provide a form of financial security, particularly for those who were aging or seeking a stable income after retirement from public service or military duty.

Annuities quickly gained popularity in Ancient Rome, especially among the elite and wealthy citizens. They were often used by individuals who wanted to ensure a guaranteed income for themselves or their families. The Roman government also utilized annuities as a means of compensating veterans and public officials, encouraging loyalty and service to the state. The structure of these early annuities was relatively simple, typically involving a contract where a person paid a sum of money to receive periodic payments for a specified period, usually for life. This financial tool allowed for risk management and financial planning in a society where other forms of social safety nets were minimal or nonexistent.

While annuities did not single-handedly build the Roman Empire, they played a significant role in its economic and social stability. By providing a reliable income stream, annuities allowed citizens to manage their finances more effectively, which contributed to economic activity and growth. The use of annuities also supported the Roman government's efforts to maintain a loyal and motivated military and administrative class, which was crucial for the empire's expansion and governance. In this way, annuities were an important financial innovation that helped underpin the economic foundation of Roman society, contributing to the empire's longevity and influence.

Wall Street is in Business for Investors

Nothing could be further from the truth. Here is the actual priority ranking:

First…for giant investment banks

Second…for selling investment products

Third…for inventing new ones to sell – based on public interest

Fourth…to profit from both sides of transactions

Fifth…for THEIR profits

Sorry, but retirees' lifetime security isn't even on the Top Ten list!

As we said in the last chapter, if this retirement investing tool was perfect, there would be no need to write this book. Everyone would already know how great annuities are and that anyone not using them would be foolish. Of course, there are downsides to every investment, and using the insurance company money market is no exception.

In this chapter, we'll dive into some of the challenges associated with this form of investing so you get the clearest picture possible. While we think using insurance company money market accounts is a great way to augment your savings for retirement, don't take our advice without doing your own legwork and research to ensure it's the right choice for your situation. Here are a few points worth considering before you decide on the best possible course.

Fees: Just like brokerage houses, insurance companies charge fees to do their work. The companies that offer these types of investment vehicles aren't doing it out of the goodness of their hearts, but rather to provide a service that is also going to benefit them in the long run. To do that, they need money to keep managing your money. By knowing the most they can about the indexes, the stocks, the economy, and all the other nitty-gritty pieces of information, they can keep offering the quality products that they do.

These fees are typically around 2%-3% per year, although they can range higher on different types of investments. 2%-3% a year might not seem bad in an account where you can't contribute more than $7,000 a year like an IRA, but what about an account with unlimited deposits? If you put $80,000 into your account in the year you open it, that 3% is $2,400. Not exactly chump change. Much like the early withdrawal on a 401(k), if you pull money from this sort of investment before age 59-½, you'll have to pay a 10% penalty tax straight to the IRS along with any money you might owe for capital gains.

We hope you never have to pull money out early, but like we said, you never know when life is going to happen and you have to take a hit in order to survive. Both vehicles have limitations for emergency situations where the 401(k) can be withdrawn early.

No Access to Funds: You have a lot of freedom with your insurance agency fund in retirement, but until you get there, you are more or less *persona non grata* in your own account. When funds go into this sort of account, you can't touch them. And if you do, you take that 10% hit. That can make life a touch uneasy if you are putting a whole lot of money into this fund early on in life when you are strapped for cash because you want it to grow into something spectacular when you get older.

Since most annuities want a major investment to get you going, this can feel unsettling if you invest $100,000 today, but suddenly need $20,000 of it next month for your father's funeral—and realize that pulling it out will cost you $22,000 plus whatever capital gains the money made. So there is obviously some need for financial diversity and longevity if you use this financial vehicle. If you put a lot of your eggs in this money market, life might get very uncomfortable before you reach age 59-½ if anything bad happens. This is why maintaining an emergency fund is crucial in your investment strategy.

The Possibility of Variable Returns: We didn't steer you wrong in the opening. There is a guaranteed rate of return for the money markets, but there are other options-that can behave a little differently. If you opt for a variable or indexed money market, you are going to incur some of the same risk. Similarly if you use a fixed rate of return and the index returns a much higher rate, you will make less money than you could have if you had just invested in the index through a traditional financial analyst.

Risk of Less Inheritance: Part of the trick here is that as you contribute more and more into your account, it will grow larger and larger based on investments you add over time. But the insurance policy you are signing up for has a finite clock attached to it, and it expires when you do…and will grow no further. That's the difference between a money market fund through an insurance company compared to a 401(k) or IRA.

If you enroll at age 63 with a big deposit of $100,000, but then you die at age 65 of a massive heart attack, your account closes on the day of your death and doesn't earn any more interest, nor do the cash payments go elsewhere unless it's under some extra add-ons. More likely, whoever you named as your beneficiary gets a lump sum payment and that is that. For most 401(k)s and IRA funds, you can name a beneficiary who can take control of the funds and that person can do whatever they want with them, including letting them stay put and grow for as long as they want.

7

The Truth About Annuities

How Do We Assemble YOUR Freedom Protection Plan®?

By far, the simplest, surest financial tool for Guaranteed Income For Life is called an annuity.

You may have heard criticism about this financial product, but most of it is unfounded. As with all criticism, just like Mom and Dad told us, we must consider the source. Most criticism of annuities comes from Wall Street people who want your money being *actively* managed by them…meaning…used for buying and selling stocks, fund shares, ETFs, even risky items like crypto…generating lush commissions and/or fees on every move and every trade, day by day. This puts your money *at risk*. This isn't so with Guaranteed Income For Life, because your money stays safely at rest inside annuities, providing you with guaranteed monthly income, and they don't like it!

However, very recently (3/24), Larry Fink, CEO of Blackrock, one of THE largest money management firms on Wall Street, a manager of billions of dollars of pension funds, shocked the world by coming out IN FAVOR OF ANNUITIES – even presenting his new plan for remaking 401(k) accounts and pension accounts to automatically transition into individually held annuities, paying – you guessed it! – GUARANTEED lifetime income, with a paycheck every month.

To be fair, annuities do have a catch, and I'll get to that in just a minute or two.

But first, a little more history. In the 1600's, European governments started using annuities and in the 1700's the British Parliament approved sale of annuities – and rich Europeans flocked to these safe harbors. **In the U.S., annuities have been available for more than TWO CENTURIES.** Actually, Social Security is a government-issued annuity, guaranteeing lifetime income, although, unfortunately, Congress has stolen its funds so its survivability is in question as early as 2026. The life insurance industry's annuities are extremely well-funded and well-administered.

People just like you rely on their annuity payments, as the solid foundation supporting other, more diversified investments, or as their entire retirement safe harbor. Either way, every month, their check arrives.

Today, there is a variety of annuities which we choose from, for your personalized Freedom Protection Plan®. Some have fixed pay-outs, some offer limited upside opportunity tied to markets along with a buffer against downside risk, some start monthly income immediately, some have a delay period to accumulate interest and raise monthly pay-out, and most have time windows where you can withdraw funds without penalties (unlike most CD's). Annuities can be TAX-ADVANTAGED, so that you LEGALLY have more tax-free retirement income. This might sound complex, but we make it simple for you, so you get exactly the financial results you want. Your plan is built to match your goals and needs. And incidentally, Wealth Express® is INDEPENDENT, not captive to any one insurer. You can rest easy, knowing that we shop for you and for the plan that's in your best interests your plan.

In many ways, figuring out your Medicare, Medicare plan B, C, D, Medicare Advantage options, choices and best plan for you is similar to figuring out your Freedom Protection Plan. Our sister company, 100Insure, has helped over 220,000 enroll in Medicare plans, and a free Medicare Check-Up is yours for the asking. We can often find ways to get you more /better benefits, lower premiums, or *both*. In developing your personal Freedom Protection Plan, we consider everything you tell us about your finances and needs and goals, and we identify the best annuities to fit perfectly. There is NO confusion.

Now, about the catch. You PURCHASE annuities. In doing so, you trade that one-time, up-front amount for the guaranteed lifetime income, but the original principal (premium payment) is no longer yours; it belongs to the annuity issuer, a large insurance company. You buy your guaranteed lifetime income stream. You can call that a catch if you want, but it actually isn't. There's nothing sneaky or tricky about it at all.

On one side, there is a package of financial safety and security, FREEDOM from active worry and market watcher anxiety—a set-it-and-forget-it investment, and guaranteed monthly income of a known, certain amount, that you can't outlive.

That's the security and certainty you've tapped into. We help you choose the best of these products for your personal Freedom Protection Plan®. On the other side, there's YOU, the customer. You buy the product for its benefits – unique exclusive benefits not matched by any other investment. That's a HUGE win-win that Wall Street can't deliver!

Why Are Annuities So Safe?

Over the past 100 years, retail investors including retirees have LOST trillions of

dollars in stock market crashes, individual companies' bankruptcies (like: General Motors, Sears, Bed, Bath & Beyond), collapsed mutual funds, even savings-and-loan and bank failures. Many people hold mutual funds, ETF's, pension accounts and don't even know what stocks are in them! Lately, the government has pressured fund managers to invest in green stocks proving to be very high risk. Some retirees make the mistake of relying entirely on their past employer's pension fund only to see their pension income suddenly slashed by 25%, even 50%. With one such famous case in Ohio, pensions were cut in half, and it took almost 6 years of litigation and an Act of Congress to get them restored.

Real estate can be almost as risky. Look at the mass migration that has recently occurred, from crime-plagued cities that were once ideal places to invest and high tax states, to Florida, Texas, and Tennessee. If an investor had his money locked up in real estate in the wrong places then, he was in trouble!

In those same 100 years, NO annuity income has stopped. Everyone with guaranteed lifetime income from annuities has been paid as agreed. Here's why:

Unlike banks, life insurance companies, by design, are NOT highly leveraged. In the 2008 Wall Street & Bank crash, Bear Stearns and Lehman Brothers were extremely highly leveraged with paper thin capital reserves as were 386 banks, and they all failed. Even as AIG's banking business crashed, its life insurance company stayed solvent and could not be raided to pay debts of its insolvent bank! Its annuity payments were never stopped. In 2023, a giant Silicon Valley Bank failed and triggered several other bank failures. During all this, no company backing annuities had the same fate.

By their corporate charters and by law, insurance companies cannot wildly speculate with customers' (policyholders') principal funds. All other investments feature speculation.

Life insurance companies are federally AND state regulated. Most states even backstop some of annuity commitments, in somewhat the same way banks have FDIC backing. Life insurance companies are the most highly regulated, most watchdogged financial institutions!

By using the safety of large numbers, life insurance companies have their risks spread over all policyholders. Their success at this kind of financial engineering is unmatched. Warren

Buffett has often said that no business matches the upside and safety of insurance companies. Even giant companies have de-risked their pensions by buying billion-dollar annuities. And top pro athletes are urged to buy annuities to prevent blowing all their money and to guarantee income after their playing days are over.

Annuities are the *Steady Eddie*. Throughout markets' ups and downs, from the Great Depression to 2008 to now, through bad recessions to sky-high inflation, throughout war and peace, the *Steady Eddie* has been annuities. Guaranteed Income For Life has never failed. With your Guaranteed For Life Plan it will feel fantastic, knowing you've made a safe, certain, reliable investment. You'll love getting that monthly retirement paycheck that shows up in your mailbox like clockwork.

A Word To The Wise

One of the great fathers of the guaranteed income strategy, Barry James Dyke, author of *Pirates of Manhattan*, a 30-year financial professional and Wall Street insider said this after the 2008 crash: *"After the greatest financial crisis since the Great Depression, Wall Street continues to* **speculate**

with your retirement savings *with reckless abandon. Only a Guaranteed Income Strategy can create the risk-free retirement income you deserve."*

Do Only "Unsophisticated" Investors Buy Annuities?

Dan S. Kennedy is the author of 36 best-selling business books including *The No B.S. Guide to Selling Your Company for Top Dollar* and *The No B.S. Guide to Wealth Attraction for Entrepreneurs*, and a popular advisor to small business owners. He says: "I am wealthy and a fairly sophisticated investor with diversified holdings in public and private companies, ETF's, corporate notes and real estate. But I still have a collection of annuities, as the solid foundation, guaranteeing me an excellent retirement income for life."

Even if other investments were wiped out, I have guaranteed income that cannot be reduced or taken away. The interest rates are comparable or superior to CD's and T-bills, but nothing else guarantees certain income for life. Frankly, I get kidded about being a scaredy-cat or grandmother investor by some of my friends and peers, but I don't care. In my mind, a certain guaranteed income is a sensible, smart piece of investment strategy even if you are a multi-millionaire – and if you are of more modest means, even more important.

There is Nothing Like The Freedom Protection Plan®!

At Wealth Express® we have made it our mission to more thoroughly understand the annuities market better than anyone, in order to use these great financial tools to create PERSONALIZED Guaranteed Income For Life for we serve. If anybody knows more about this than we do, we'd like to meet them!

When you have YOUR Freedom Protection Plan® in place, you can finally RELAX ABOUT MONEY. There's nothing else that can provide *that*.

And remember, YOUR Freedom Protection Plan can be created for you with NO COST, NO OBLIGATION and NEVER, EVER, EVER ANY SALES PRESSURE. The *Wealth Express® Certified Advisor* you'll meet with must sign our Integrity Pledge and meet definitive qualifications. No one is ever judgmental about your finances. If, for example, you have scattered investments bought at different times from different sources, you are not alone! If you are at risk without fully understanding it, you are not alone! We are here to help you get it all organized, under firm control, and SIMPLIFIED. Your conversation with us is absolutely private and confidential.

Call 833-600-2832 now

to schedule your FREE Retirement Risk Assessment Meeting with a Wealth Express® Certified Advisor.

WSA 132

8

Imagine the Perfect Retirement…

Retirement is different for everyone, but there are two essential things everyone wants.

The first is **time**.

The second is **freedom**.

You don't have much spare time for yourself

and your own pursuits during those decades of full-time work. You end up making a lot of sacrifices for others - your spouse, children, parents, and job. We do it out of love and commitment, and because that's God's command for us to be a good Christian person.

But if you let it all go without stopping to smell the roses, what are you working so hard for? When the time comes to retire, you want to enjoy your golden years. Maybe you want to travel, spend time with loved ones, learn a new skill, read, write, take care of the grandkids; it can take any form you want! With your Guaranteed Income For Life plan, you get to decide what to do in retirement; you get to define what your retirement identity looks like. And doing that will feel incredible!

The second is freedom. The freedom to do what you want, when you want it. That's something that millions of Americans don't get to enjoy in retirement because they never found the path to financial freedom. They wind up living in a disappointing senior living facility or the home they've owned for 60 years that is falling apart in a neighborhood where the property values are going down while the crime rate steadily goes up. They have a lifestyle of barely making ends meet every month—and that's only if they are extremely conservative on what they eat and where, what they buy, and where they shop. Vacations are out of the question. Visits with the family only occur when their children and grandkids have time to come to them. A new car is not in the cards and housing repairs transition from essential to almost impossible. These struggles are painful to see someone we love to suffer through.

You swear it will never happen to you, only to see it happen because you didn't know about Guaranteed Income For Life and bet the farm that the stock market would do better. You thought you had more time and secretly hoped you could save A LOT near the end of your working days.

That's not the future you deserve. Your future is one where you have the freedom to take the trip to Paris you've been promising yourself since you were in college. The freedom to enjoy a second honeymoon and upgrade your wife's wedding ring. It's the freedom to start a college fund for your grandchild before they even take their first step, giving them the biggest advantage anyone can have in life. It's the freedom to decide that at age 75, you've earned the right to splurge on season tickets to your favorite sports team.

My point is the range of choices doesn't matter; the only thing that does is the freedom to decide what YOU want and what YOUR retirement identity looks like. And knowing that freedom is yours will be amazing!

The best part of it all is that with Guaranteed Income for Life, you'll never run out of money. Ever. Because your principal keeps compounding throughout your lifetime. This isn't a 401(k) account where you're guessing how long you will live. This will never be your story: *"I thought I'd live to 85, but now I'm 93 and broke - should I be disappointed in my good health?"* The money will keep building in your annuity, and upon your passing, it will pay out any outstanding debts you have to the insurance company. Then the rest will go to your heirs, to help make their transition to life without you as smooth and comfortable as possible.

Guaranteed Income for Life makes that happen. And it gives you peace of mind in every retirement year, so each year is worry free and sweeter than you ever thought possible.

9

Watcher Anxiety, The Worst Way To Live

This is a 100% true story that happened to me when I was a kid. My dad had secured a nice job that gave him a lot of stock options in the oil company he worked for. That company was booming throughout the 1980s and he was making a killing—despite struggling to graduate from college. He decided to take some of the money and invest in a few other companies to see how he could do. He wasn't going to go broke doing this; it was only a pastime, or so we thought.

Eventually he chose 3-4 other stocks; I have no idea how, probably from reading magazines since we were still 10-15 years away from the Internet. I really liked spending time with my Dad, so eventually I would get up early, get the business section out of the morning paper, and see how his stocks were doing. He had taught me how to read the stock page, identify the symbols, and read the high-low data, PE ratios, etc. His employer's stock was frequently on the rise, but the other ones were up and down like a rollercoaster.

One day, he added a fourth, company he had heard about on the radio, a tiny little startup called *Priam* that was on the *NASDAQ* and sold hard drives. Despite what my Dad had heard, *Priam* was not doing well. It turned out they were losing money hand over fist. And as we watched the prices steadily drop over time, my dad would grow more and more agitated. I stopped looking at the paper before he got up, because more often than not he'd ask me for the prices—I distinctly remember the sounds of my dad swearing and smacking his fist into the kitchen table one morning when he'd found *Priam* had vanished because the company had declared bankruptcy.

Let's remember that this was just a hobby for my dad, not an investment he was counting on, but it took a huge toll on his mental and emotional well-being. Watcher anxiety - the condition people get when they start obsessing about their financial investments—can chew you up with agonizing fear, haunt you with the notion that you've screwed everything up. It fills you with a-growing sense of panic that you have to act now and get out of this terrible this terrible situation before it is too late.

The Guaranteed Income for Life plan ends your need to obsess about individual stocks, the Dow Jones, the S&P 500, NASDAQ or any other financial index. Your agreement is with an insurance company, and they've been making it their business for more than a century to guarantee that in exchange for your trust, you'll always get consistent payouts and the ability to borrow against the insurance company's principal anytime you want.

Call 833-600-2832 now

to schedule your FREE Retirement Risk Assessment Meeting with a Wealth Express® Certified Advisor.

WSA 133

10

Wall Street's Ignorance

Here's the thing that your Wall Street broker hopes you will never find out: their retirement portfolio probably looks nothing like what they are trying to sell you. Oh, they'll tell you about the stocks they're investing in, but I guarantee that if you asked to see their financial portfolio they would stammer out something like, *"That's not appropriate." or "I'm not allowed to."* And yeah, it's not really appropriate to ask someone about their finances, but it also allows them to never have to tell the truth. When you ask a Wall Street investment broker about annuities, you'll probably get one of two reactions: Either they will play dumb and act like they don't know what it is since the company doesn't offer it, or they will spend the next 10-15 minutes telling you why annuities are such a bad idea.

If you're this far into the book, you probably already know what their reasons will be, but I'll go ahead and share the real reason Wall Street people don't like annuities: They don't make any money off of them.

That's it. And yes, that's a greedy reason isn't it? That doesn't sound like the voice of the person who told you that they want to guide you through your financial journey and they're always there to help. If that was the case, they'd investigate every single opportunity available to you, not just the ones that make them and their employers rich.

If you pick an annuity, your investment broker doesn't make any money off you. All your fees go right to the insurance company. Those fees are proven to maintain your account and everything about the fund. On the other hand, the fees charged by an investment firm are sketchy at best. A lot of them sound like they are doing the same thing, but you are getting charged two or three times anyway. When you go through the investment firm, they act like they're the *Great and Powerful Oz* and you're the *Cowardly Lion* quivering at their feet, begging for your help. When you go with a Guaranteed Income for Life plan, you're the one running the show. The insurance company works for you.

It's a shame Wall Street thinks that way, because offering annuities would do wonders for both you and the investment broker, especially when you consider these points:

#1 Taxes: If you use an IRA or a 401(k), you'll get taxed to death either at the time of deposit or when you pull money out. A 401(k) also gets taxed three different times when it transfers to someone else after your demise. With an annuity, you pay taxes once.

#2 Liquidity: Have you ever tried to pull money out of an IRA or 401(k) before you turned 59-½? I have, and it's like trying to get a gold bar out of Fort Knox. You get reprimanded for taking money out early, you have to sign a document saying you're aware of the penalty you'll incur, and then it takes forever to get the money. With an annuity, you can borrow any amount that you can cover at any time.

#3 Deposit Limitations: It continues to hurt my brain that IRAs and 401(k)s have limitations on how much you can put into your account in a single year. In 2024, those numbers were $23,000 for a 401(k) and $7,500 for an IRA. The official reason from the IRS is that it makes sure that higher-paid employees can't take advantage of the tax benefits. Wow, God forbid people making high salaries should want to save a lot of money. IRS regulations make me want to throw my hands up in the air! However, there are no limitations for your annuity. If your great uncle leaves you $250,000 after he passes away, you are free to pour it all in there anytime you want.

#4: No guarantees on money: You could put the IRS-mandated maximum of $23,000 a year into a 401(k) for 40 years if you wanted to. That would be a total contribution of $920,000. If you actually got the mythical 10% rate of return every year on that money, you'd have $11.2 million by the time you were 62. That's never happened to anyone ever. Because the market goes up and down like a yo-yo. If the true rate of return was 5% over those 40 years, guess how much money you'd lose from the first total? More than $8 million! Your actual total would be $2.94 million, and even that's not guaranteed because your principal will go up and down as years go boom or bust. With annuities, your interest rate is guaranteed to grow at the same rate every year, even if the market crashes. You might feel a little FOMO when you make 4-6% when the market booms and returns a 20% rate of return on the S&P 500. But compare that to how fantastic you'll feel when it returns -35% and everyone you know has pushed the panic button.

Everyone, of course, but you. While they all lament their vanished dividend checks, you'll be getting your steady retirement paycheck every month for the rest of your life, just like you did when you were working.

11

The Ultimate Annuity Loophole

We are wary of loopholes, aren't we? Either they're a scam or too good to be true. Or the minute we try it, the IRS shows up at our door with a warrant. However, there is an annuity tax loophole that works every time if you know what you are doing. Purchasing an annuity is a tax-deferred way to increase your retirement savings.

There's no limit on how much you can contribute each year, and you're only penalized if you withdraw money early.

Since you can take out a loan from the insurance company, this never needs to be a problem. Because this is a retirement account, all of the money you earn each year on interest, dividends, and capital gains are reinvested every year... Which means you're not being taxed on them. Even more exciting is what happens if you buy a non-qualified annuity.

A non-qualified annuity is purchased with after-tax dollars, meaning you've already paid taxes on that money. You can use a regular savings account or a money market account to do this. Since you've already been taxed on those dollars, it won't happen again. You also can take advantage of something called *the exclusion ratio*, which is defined as the portion of your contribution to the annuity that is taxed upon withdrawal. The *exclusion ratio* determines what the earnings are for the annuity since it didn't get taxed. Taxes have to be paid when you withdraw the money, but earnings grow tax-free until then.

Every year, your 401(k) is charging you tax dollars for money that you don't see and that you might never see depending on how the stock market rises and falls over time. Nobody should be charged on dollars that they'll never actually have! The annuity loophole allows you to avoid taxes on all the yearly gains you're making, saving you an enormous amount of money. The tax bill comes when you withdraw your money in retirement—but that's to be expected, and this format guarantees you'll only get taxed once on your money. That's not a loophole, that's a winning strategy that gives you the certainty you deserve in your golden years!

Call 833-600-2832 now

to schedule your FREE Retirement Risk Assessment Meeting with a Wealth Express® Certified Advisor.

WSA 134

12

Who Do You Want to Be in Retirement?

It's somewhat of a bitter coincidence that we've arrived at Chapter 11, because a lot of people who don't handle their retirement finances correctly end up filing for Chapter 11.

The question posed in this chapter's title—about what **your retirement identity** will look like—is important. It will define the choices you make regarding investing your money going forward.

Who do you want to be in retirement?

If your answer is a hermit on a desert island, well, thanks for reading but you don't need us! If your answer is a little more interesting, like becoming a traveler, wine taster, a sports car collector, or an always-available grandparent—well now you're talking! Dream big and you'll find your way to big things.

Because before you can think about how much money you'll need in retirement, you need to picture what that life looks like. Don't hold back! Think about the things you've always wanted to do but never got the chance, or think about the things you love doing that you never seem to have enough time for.

Do you want to travel the world and see all the amazing things that were previously limited to the Internet, TV, or the movies?

Do you want to reconnect with friends and family and spend more time remembering the past and making new memories for the future?

Do you want to become a connoisseur of great literature, works of art, and food from around the world?

There is no wrong answer except for the one that permanently limits you. The one that has you putting off your annual physical a few more months because you can't afford the copay. The one that demands you must- stretch your $100 weekly grocery budget to make ends meet. The one where you set the air conditioner to 82 degrees instead of 72 or wrap yourself in extra blankets in winter so you don't have to run the heater so high.

Our Retirement Risk Assessment Meeting will show you exactly where you stand, to see if your current savings match your dreams, or if there is a gap between where you are and where you want to be.

Financial constraints force us into difficult choices that sometimes becomes impossible choices. What's more important…refilling my medicine or having enough food in the house? Fixing the car's engine or the hole in my roof?

We never want to see anyone suffer. And the worst sight of all is to see someone who worked hard for decades having to move out of their nice home into a third-tier senior community with a roommate. That because of bad-financial choices, they don't have *nearly* the amount of money they thought they would.

It happens every day. People are forced to move in with their kids because they can't afford the mortgage. People at age 70 and 75 and beyond going back to work at low-paying, menial, part-time jobs so they can keep the power on or not have their car repossessed.

We all fear that late life vision of ourselves. The good news is that the worry-free retirement of your dreams is within reach… but you can't be passive about it. Getting there successfully requires immediate action and careful planning, starting **NOW**. Guaranteed Income for Life is the next step you need to take to make your beautiful retirement dreams come true.

13

The Next Step

You've made it to the end of this book, but this is not the ending…

…It's the beginning. The start of your time to get on the sure path to your dream retirement. To a certain, solid, reliable retirement paycheck. The most reliable income stream that's possible. One you can lock now in by taking advantage of the best financial opportunity of your *life*.

Why not pick up the phone and call us directly, and schedule a free, no-obligation meeting with a *Wealth Express® Certified Advisor* to discuss your Guaranteed Income For Life plan? The expert Advisor can show whether or not you are ready for retirement or at risk. It takes only two minutes and will give you a clear answer on whether your savings match your retirement dreams. It puts you on the path towards certainty in a very uncertain world.

It's time to unlock your certain financial future and control how you'll achieve your retirement dreams. We're here to help you make the right decisions for YOU; not for us, and certainly not for some fee-happy Wall Street investment firm that only wants your money because it helps them make more money.

This is the path forward toward a worry-free retirement the financial freedom to do the things you've always dreamt about. The traditional 401(k) or IRA route is risky, uncertain, and only provides the chance to gamble with Wall Street and wind up with far less than you put in. Please don't do that to yourself! Take the sure path that leads to a consistent monthly retirement paycheck that always shows up while you are relaxing and enjoying your golden years.

Remember, you'll have the right to borrow money any time you need, and Guaranteed Income for Life is an investment that's certain and compounds yearly. You'll have the peace of mind that at the end of the line, you've set up the most important people in your life with a generous legacy gift. One that they don't have to worry about, now or in the future. It's the greatest gift you can give to yourself and to your family. Why wait another minute?

Call 833-600-2832 now

to schedule your FREE Retirement Risk Assessment Meeting with a Wealth Express® Certified Advisor.

WSA 135

Made in the USA
Columbia, SC
29 October 2024